TEAMMATES FOR LIFE

written by Sarah Bird

illustrated by Cynthia McGrellis

**McGraw-Hill
School Division**

New York   Farmington

Let's say you join a team this year. Now imagine you are on the same team when you have your own kids. Let's go even further— what if you are still on the team when you have grandchildren?

There really is a team like this. It's a group of men in their fifties. They still meet to play the same game that they played together more than 40 years ago!

The game is called stickball. Stickball is a
kind of baseball that kids who lived in New
York City used to play. They played it
because all you needed was a broomstick for
a bat and a little pink rubber ball.

You didn't need gloves to play stickball. Lots of kids didn't have them. You didn't need other things that cost a lot of money like uniforms, bats, or baseballs.

You didn't need coaches, bases, or even a field to play stickball. Most kids played stickball in the street.

Yiggy, Fuzzy, Moe, Dizzy, Murray and Sam and the others who played with them lived in a part of New York City called the Bronx.

They called themselves "SEMANON," which is NO NAMES spelled backwards.

The Semanons had a kind of field to play in. It was the playground of P.S. 95, the school they went to. They still play stickball in the same field.

When they were children these boys played stickball together after school almost every day. Now they are grown up and have their own kids.

They get together once a year, in June, to play stickball.

Stickball is fun. Lots of times the Semanons would play a kind of stickball called "automatics." In that game you didn't run around the bases.

If you hit the ball over the playground fence, it was a two-base hit. If the ball touched the second floor of the building across from the school, you went to third base. If your hit stretched to the third floor, you scored a point.

Stickball was great, but it was only a small part of what still makes these men a team.

Some of them still live in the Bronx neighborhood where they grew up. Some live thousands of miles from each other.

But whenever they need something or something bad happens to one of them, they can always count on other Semanons to help.

When one of the friends is sick, the others send cards, call on the telephone, and ask if they can help in any way. When one of them needs money, others will offer to give it—even if they do not have much themselves.

Whenever something good happens to one of them, they can be sure other Semanons will be there to celebrate.

When a Semanon kid gets married, the others come to the wedding. When a Semanon gets a great new job, they throw a party.

If one of the group is moving, he doesn't call a moving company to come with a big truck—he calls his friends!

Yiggy, Fuzzy, Moe and the other Semanons do lots of things together. They take trips to Pennsylvania to play golf. They go to watch the pros play baseball, football, and other sports. They go to concerts and movies together.

This team sounds like a family, doesn't it? How did they get to be so close? And why have they stayed so close for so long?

The Semanons grew up together in a special way. Cooperation was the way they grew up. Cooperation is another name for teamwork.

They all lived in two big buildings in the same neighborhood.

In these apartment houses, called co-ops (this comes from the word cooperation), every family owned a part of their building.

People owned their apartments in the buildings where Yiggy, Fuzzy, and the others grew up. But they also owned a part of the halls, the stairs, the basement, the roof, the furnace, and the yard. That encouraged everyone to help keep the building looking nice.

People had lots of meetings about how to fix problems in these apartment houses.

Sharing also helped everyone to get to know each other. People in the building became friends. They were able to count on each other when they needed help.

Of course, to have good teamwork, you need people who care almost as much about the whole group as they care about themselves.

The parents of the boys in the Semanons were like that. They chose to live where they could share some of the work and be good neighbors.

There were other kinds of teamwork in the buildings where the Semanons grew up.

The people in the buildings started a summer day camp and a nursery school for the children. Parents and other grown-ups in the building worked in the camp and the school.

Yiggy is 56 years old now. His real name is Edward Yeager. He says he was lucky to grow up with all that sharing, teamwork, and friendship.

He says it made him and his friends believe that sharing, teamwork, and friendships are the most important things in life.

Yiggy and some of the Semanons still live in the old neighborhood in New York. Some live all the way across the country.

A few of them are teachers. Some are doctors, or dentists, or lawyers. A couple of them work in banks or with computers.

But when they think about how much they care about each other, these differences are small. They are teammates for life.